BLUE TITS

Sally Morgan

W
FRANKLIN WATTS
LONDON•SYDNEY

© 2005 Franklin Watts
First published in 2005
by Franklin Watts
96 Leonard Street
London EC2A 4XD

Franklin Watts Australia
45-51 Huntley Street
Alexandria NSW 2015

Produced for Franklin Watts by
White-Thomson Publishing Ltd
210 High Street
Lewes BN7 2NH

Editor: Rachel Minay
Designed by: Tinstar Design Ltd
Picture research: Morgan Interactive Ltd
Consultant: Frank Blackburn
Printed in: China

**British Library Cataloguing
in Publication Data**
A CIP catalogue record for this book is
available from the British Library.

ISBN: 0 7496 6068 6

Acknowledgements
The publishers would like to thank
the following for permission to
reproduce these photographs:

Corbis
7 (Corbis/Frank Lane/Ronald Thompson),
25 (Corbis/Frank Lane/Mike Jones);

Ecoscene
4–5 (Annie Poole), 10 (Frank Blackburn),
11 (Steve Austin), 12 (Laura Sivell),
13 (Hugh Clarke), 16 (Robert Nichol),
17 (Pete Cairns), 20 (Bryan Knox),
21 (Frank Blackburn), 27 (Alan Towse),
28 (Phillip Marazzi), 29 (William
Middleton);

Nature Picture Library
FC, 1 (T J Rich), 6 (Mike Wilkes),
8 (Dave Watts), 9 (Terry Andrewartha),
14 (William Osborn), 15 (George
McCarthy), 18 (Ross Hoddinott),
19 (William Osborn), 22 (Chris O'Reilly),
23 (William Osborn), 24 (Mike Beynon),
26 (Bernard Castelein).

Every effort has been made to contact copyright
holders of any material reproduced in this book.
Any omissions will be rectified in subsequent
printings if notice is given to the publishers.

Contents

The blue tit

The blue tit is one of the best-known birds in Britain. It is also one of the most colourful with its blue, yellow and black feathers.

It is difficult to know whether this is a male or female blue tit as they look very similar.

blue wings

blue tail

blue crown

dark stripe
around the eye

beak

yellow breast

feet

Blue tits are birds

The blue tit is a small bird. Its body is covered with feathers and it has two wings. It lays eggs, out of which young birds, called chicks, hatch.

Perching birds

Blue tits belong to a group of birds called perching birds, or passerines, because they have a foot with four toes. Three toes face forwards and one faces backwards. This arrangement allows the blue tit to grip a twig firmly and perch. The blue tit's toes grip the twig even while the bird is asleep!

VITAL **STATISTICS**

- ▸ *The body of a blue tit is 11–12 cm long.*
- ▸ *Its wing span is 15–20 cm.*
- ▸ *It weighs 9.5–12.5 g.*
- ▸ *Its life span is four to five years, but can be as much as 21 years.*
- ▸ *Its Latin name is* **Parus caeruleus.**

Making a nest

Male and female blue tits come together in March, to form pairs and mate.

Building a nest

The pair of blue tits build their nest in a small hole in a tree, a crevice in a wall or in a bird box. The nest is made from a range of materials such as grass, hair, wool and moss. The female lines the inside of the nest with feathers taken from her own body.

animal CLUES

Watch out for pairs of blue tits collecting nesting materials in the garden. Put out some nesting materials, such as pieces of cotton wool, feathers and moss, and see if they are collected by birds.

These blue tits are collecting wool caught on a fence to use in their nest.

A blue tit egg is smooth, glossy and white with reddish-brown spots. It is about 16 mm by 12 mm.

Incubating eggs

By April or May, the female is ready to lay her eggs. Each day she lays one egg, until there is a clutch of about 10 to 12 eggs. Once they are all laid, the female sits on her eggs to keep them warm. This is called incubation. She incubates her eggs for between 12 and 14 days. During this time the male brings her food. She leaves the nest for short periods of time to drink, bathe and clean her feathers.

ANIMAL **FACTS**

▶ *One record-breaking blue tit nest was found to contain a clutch of 24 eggs.*

Growing up

Blue tit chicks hatch from the eggs without any feathers and their eyes are closed. They are completely helpless and must be kept warm.

Feeding the chicks

The parents have to work hard as they raise their chicks. The chicks grow quickly and demand lots of food. The parents fly to and from the nest with a supply of caterpillars to feed their hungry chicks.

ANIMAL FACTS

▶ *On average, a pair of blue tits gather one caterpillar every minute to feed their hungry chicks.*

Chicks grow quickly and they have huge appetites.

8

Flying the nest

The chicks soon grow their feathers and this helps to keep them warm. By the time they are about three weeks old they are ready to leave the nest. The only way to leave the nest is by flying. Often the mother sits on a nearby branch with a caterpillar to encourage the young birds, known as fledglings.

This fledgling has just flown from the nest and is perching on a nearby branch.

Where do blue tits live?

Blue tits are found all over Britain, from the northernmost part of Scotland (except the islands of Orkney and Shetland) to Cornwall.

Blue tit habitats

Blue tits live in a number of different types of habitat. Once they were found mostly in woodlands and hedgerows, where they could find nesting sites in trees. Now they are found in parks and gardens too. They are among the most common birds in the garden.

Blue tits can find plenty of nesting sites and food in woodlands.

Blue tits can be seen feeding in many gardens throughout Britain.

Winter visitors

In winter the numbers of blue tits in the south and east of England increases when blue tits from other parts of Europe fly over the English Channel. The weather is warmer in Britain and there is more food for the birds.

Flight

Birds have wings and their bodies are covered in feathers. Birds, bats and insects are the only animals that can fly.

Feathers

The blue tit has three types of feather. It has long stiff feathers on its wings called flight feathers. Covering its body are smaller softer feathers called contour feathers, which give the bird a smooth covering and outline. This helps it to slip through the air as it flies. Close to its skin is a layer of tiny down feathers, which trap heat and help to keep the bird warm.

The body of a bird is covered in a layer of feathers.

Blue tits take off rapidly and can dodge sideways to avoid predators.

Flapping flight

Birds fly by flapping their wings up and down, using powerful chest muscles. They tend to fly short distances, for example from branch to branch in the garden, but they can fly over longer distances too.

Blue tits are among the most acrobatic of birds as they can hang upside down on branches and bird feeders.

ANIMAL **FACTS**

▶ **The blue tit flies at speeds of up to 20 km/h.**

Blue tit food

Blue tits eat a mix of plant and animal food so they are called omnivores. Their diet changes through the year as some foods become available and others disappear.

Feeding on caterpillars

In summer there are plenty of green caterpillars in the garden. These are one of the blue tits' favourite foods and they feed them to their young. Blue tits also hunt for other insect larvae as well as adult butterflies and moths. In the garden they search among the plants and in crevices for greenflies, beetles and spiders.

In autumn there are fewer insects around, so blue tits feed on seeds and fruits. They find these foods in gardens and along hedgerows. They land on sunflower heads and pull out the seeds.

Blue tits eat many caterpillars each day in summer.

Short beaks

The shape of the blue tit's beak is designed for feeding on a variety of foods. It is short and thick and able to cope with cracking seeds and nuts, as well as picking up small insects such as greenfly.

ANIMAL **FACTS**

▶ *Blue tits and other tits often peck at the putty around windows, especially in winter. They may be attracted to the linseed oil in the putty, though it is more likely that they are simply searching for food.*

Blue tits feed on fallen fruits in autumn.

Blue tits have enemies

Blue tits are small birds and are preyed upon by a number of larger birds and mammals.

Predators

The blue tit's main predators are grey squirrels, great spotted woodpeckers and magpies. These predators can reach into the nest and pull out blue tit chicks. They eat any eggs that they find, too.

The adult blue tits may also be preyed upon by birds of prey, such as sparrowhawks.

The feet of the great spotted woodpecker are able to grip the tree trunk, allowing the bird to pull chicks from blue tit nests.

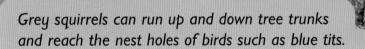

Grey squirrels can run up and down tree trunks and reach the nest holes of birds such as blue tits.

Crashing into glass

Blue tits and other garden birds may be killed when they fly into the glass of windows or patio doors. They do not see the glass. This can be prevented by placing stickers on the glass to make it more visible. Paper silhouettes of birds of prey on the glass scare away garden birds.

Senses

Birds need good senses to survive. They need to find plenty of food and avoid predators. Their sight is most useful to them. It gives information about their surroundings as they fly from branch to branch.

ANIMAL **FACTS**

▶ *Some birds, including blue tits, see ultraviolet light. This helps them find berries and other food.*

Blue tits rely on sight to spot danger from predators.

The blue tit has a pair of nostrils on the top of its beak, but its sense of smell is quite poor, so it relies on sight to find food.

Good eyesight

Birds have colour vision, like humans, so they can pick out berries and other food among green leaves. Their eyes can see fine detail, which means they are able to spot small insects such as greenfly on branches. They are particularly good at detecting movement. As their eyes are on the sides of their head, they have a wide angle of vision to spot predators flying in from the side or from above.

science LINKS

How wide is your field of view? Try this out to see if you could spot a predator creeping up from your left side. Stand with your back to a friend and ask them to hold a pencil about a metre from your left ear. Looking straight ahead, can you see the pencil in the corner of your eye? If not, ask your friend to move it forwards until you can see it.

19

Blue tit song

Birds use their calls and songs to communicate with each other.

Trilling song

The song of the blue tit can be heard for many months of the year, although hardly ever during the winter as the days are short and the birds are not breeding. Male blue tits have a trilling song, *tsee-tsee-tsu-hu-hu-hu-hu*, which starts in January before the breeding season.

animal CLUES

The best time to hear birdsong is at dawn in early May. You will need to get up at about 5 a.m. and go outside to listen to all the different birds singing. The birdsong usually starts with the blackbird singing, followed by the song thrush. Gradually more birds of various species join in.

The blue tit uses song to attract a mate.

Making sounds

The sounds are made by the syrinx – a type of voice box near the lungs. Sounds are produced when air flows through the narrow passage of the syrinx and causes a membrane to vibrate, just like a drum skin vibrates when it is hit.

Learning to sing

Birds are born with a basic ability to sing, but they also copy their parents' calls and songs, and those of other mature birds. A young bird starts to learn to sing with a jumble of notes. In time it adds notes and finally produces a song.

Blue tits use sound to warn other birds away. Their alarm call is a churring sound. If this fails, blue tits may fight.

Surviving winter

Winter is a tough time for birds. The days are short and the weather is cold. There is little food around for birds and water is often frozen.

Keeping warm

Birds need to eat food every day. When food is broken down inside a bird's body, it releases heat that keeps the body warm. A bird can help to insulate its body by fluffing up its feathers. This traps air between the feathers and reduces the amount of heat that is lost to the environment.

In severe weather blue tits take shelter in holes in trees or in nest boxes. Inside they get protection from wind, rain and the cold.

This blue tit is sheltering from cold weather in a bird nesting box.

science LINKS

Air is a good insulator. Some clothing, such as a jacket, has air trapped in a fluffy lining between two layers of fabric. A house has layers of insulation in the loft to trap warm air below. Many homes also have double-glazed windows; two panes of glass with an air space in between.

Blue tits search for food

In the winter months, blue tits join up with other small birds to form flocks that fly between trees and from shrub to shrub searching for seeds, fruits and insects.

Flocks of blue tits and great tits visit bird feeders in winter in search of food.

Clever birds

Birds are very adaptable and they can learn new behaviour. They have moved into towns and cities where they can find food and places to build nests.

Blue tits are intelligent

Blue tits are very clever. They have learnt how to find food in gardens. Often they are the first visitors to a new bird table. Blue tits are small and acrobatic so they can land on hanging bird feeders. They soon find out how to pull out the nuts.

ANIMAL **FACTS**

▸ *The blue tit is one of six species of tit in Britain. The largest is the great tit, which looks similar to the blue tit. It has a black head and neck.*

This blue tit has learnt that to reach the peanuts it must pull out the matchstick.

Blue tits have learnt to drink cream from milk bottles left on front doorsteps by pecking through the foil cap on the bottle. Small birds such as blue tits like to feed on cream because it contains a lot of fat. Fatty foods are high in energy and this helps the birds to keep warm, especially during the winter months.

Many people get annoyed when they find that the blue tit has stolen all the cream from their milk!

Attracting blue tits

There are many ways of attracting blue tits into a garden so you can see them close up.

Blue tits like pecking at balls of fat hung from branches.

Bird food

The easiest way is to put out food that blue tits like to eat. They prefer to hang onto bird feeders and bags rather than land on a flat bird table. So hanging bags of peanuts and fat balls are ideal. Keep the bird feeder well stocked with food. Birds may rely on the food that you put out when they can't find food elsewhere. Remember that birds need water too, especially in cold weather when water may be frozen.

science LINKS

Find out which food is liked best by different birds. Place a selection of bird foods on a bird table and watch which birds feed on them. Most birds have a favourite food.

Putting up a nesting box is a good way of attracting blue tits into your garden.

Nest boxes

Blue tits need places to build their nests and will readily choose a nest box. However, it has to be the right type. Nest boxes for blue tits have a small entrance hole that other birds, especially magpies, cannot squeeze through.

ANIMAL **FACTS**

▶ *Watch out for cats in the garden. British cats are thought to kill more than 55 million birds each year. The most frequently caught are house sparrows, blue tits, blackbirds and starlings.*

Bird stories

The blue tit's name

In the past the blue tit was called the blue titmouse. The word titmouse simply means 'little bird'. All the tits were called titmouse or titmice. Since this was quite a long word, it soon got shortened to 'tit'. Some surnames, such as Titmuss and Titmarsh, are named after these birds.

Birds are often seen as a sign of spring or of good or bad luck.

The sound of the cuckoo calling is a sign of spring. In parts of Scotland, it is lucky to hear the cuckoo if you are out walking but not before you have eaten breakfast.

The arrival of the swallows in spring is a sign to put away your winter clothing.

Many people think it is unlucky to see a single crow or a magpie but it is lucky to see two.

These are very old myths about different birds.

A barn owl perched on a house was thought to be unlucky and meant that someone inside was going to die.

Ravens have been linked to the Tower of London since the 13th century. They are kept there because of a legend that says if the ravens disappear, then Britain will be invaded.

Some people believed that birds had magical powers and that the heart of an owl would cure blindness.

Blue tit facts

The Tit family

The blue tit belongs to the family of tits. There are about 50 species of tit in the world. They are found in North and Central America, Europe, Africa and Asia. The six species of British tit are the great, coal, crested, marsh, willow and blue tit.

MAIN FEATURES OF THE BLUE TIT

- *The blue tit is a bird with feathers and wings.*
- *It is one of the most common garden birds.*
- *It nests in holes in trees and walls, and in bird boxes.*
- *The female lays 10–12 eggs which hatch after 12–14 days.*
- *Young blue tits leave the nest after about three weeks.*
- *It feeds on caterpillars, seeds and nuts, and insects such as greenfly and beetles.*
- *The blue tit is preyed upon by grey squirrels, woodpeckers, magpies and sparrowhawks.*

Did you know…?

Blue tits nest in many strange places such as disused letterboxes and pipes.

Blue tit websites

Royal Society for the Protection of Birds (RSPB)

www.rspb.org.uk
Informative website that features all the British birds.

Garden Birds

www.garden-birds.co.uk
Website that provides information on birds that come into the garden.

Note to parents and teachers: Every effort has been made by the publishers to ensure that these websites are suitable for children; that they are of the highest educational value, and that they contain no inappropriate or offensive material. However, because of the nature of the Internet, it is impossible to guarantee that the contents of these sites will not be altered. We strongly advise that Internet access is supervised by a responsible adult.

Glossary

acrobatic agile, able to swing and turn upside down on branches

adaptable able to get used to

bird of prey a predatory bird, such as an eagle, osprey or falcon, that has a hooked beak and powerful claws

caterpillar the larval stage of a butterfly or moth

chick a young bird

clutch a group of eggs in a nest incubated by a bird

egg the object laid by a bird that a chick hatches out of

habitat the home of an animal or plant

hatch break open or emerge from an egg

incubate keep eggs warm

insulate cover something to keep it warm

insulator something that keeps in heat

mate reproduce

membrane a thin layer or sheet, for example a layer of cells

myths old stories from a long time ago

nesting materials items used to build a nest such as leaves, wool and moss

omnivore an animal that eats a mixed diet of plants and meat

perching sitting on a branch

predator an animal that hunts other animals

prey on/upon hunt

syrinx the vocal cords of a bird, found near the lungs

ultraviolet a colour that humans cannot see, although insects and many birds can

Index